My Unpacked Suitcase

My Unpacked Suitcase

LynnDee Wilks

Xulon Press

Xulon Press
2301 Lucien Way #415
Maitland, FL 32751
407.339.4217
www.xulonpress.com

© 2017 by LynnDee Wllks

All rights reserved solely by the author. The author guarantees all contents are original and do not infringe upon the legal rights of any other person or work. No part of this book may be reproduced in any form without the permission of the author. The views expressed in this book are not necessarily those of the publisher.

Scripture quotations taken from the Holy Bible, New International Version (NIV). Copyright © 1973, 1978, 1984, 2011 by Biblica, Inc.™. Used by permission. All rights reserved.

Edited by Xulon Press.

Printed in the United States of America.

ISBN-13: 9781545610473

This book is dedicated to:

My Savior in heaven, for grace and for shining
Your light for me to follow.
Shawn Michael, my steady hand to hold, my love,
and my soulmate.
Dad, for your huge love and guidance.
Mom, for your beauty and kindness inside and out,
and for showing me adventure
Rolly, Every little sister needs a big brother to
teach her how to fight.
Kaegen, my greatest gift.
Sammi, Demi, and Emalie, my "bonus" daughters.
Mamma Linda and Captain,
My Swiss family and my tribe.
"Love wins every time."
Debi Capito-Young, for your
inspiration and encouragement.

Table of Contents

This book is dedicated to: v

Introduction ix

The Early Days 1

Beauty in Nature 8

Let's Go Back, but Not Stay Long 12

Time for a Bath 20

Not Just a Leaf 24

A New Start 28

In the Low Times, We Find Our Answers 35

She Believed She Could So She Did 39

Some Things Are Worth Remembering, ...45

My Perspective from Behind the Chair 49

Bread Crumbs 55

He Shows Up 60

Life Lesson's Learned the Hard Way 65

About the Author 69

Photographs 71

Introduction

My life feels like a giant puzzle that God has given me the little pieces for. Now we are assembling it *together*. Piece by piece, I step back and am in awe of His timing and the huge part He plays in each day. It's difficult for me to relinquish control, but now that I have, I am amazed at the way He shapes and guides my path. "Call to me and I will answer you and tell you great and unsearchable things you do not know" (Jeremiah 33:3).

The Early Days

When I was a little girl, my dad would tell me that he climbed to the top of the mountain and special-ordered a blonde-haired, blue-eyed, freckle-faced little girl with dimples straight from God, and that's exactly what he got. I loved that story. "Dad, tell me again how you ordered me from God," I would say. My dad had a way of making me feel like I was truly his answer to prayer.

I grew up with two older half brothers in a small town in the Northwest. We spent most of our weekends at our cabin along the banks of the Snake River in Hells Canyon. It remains our little piece of heaven on earth. I still try to get there every weekend to escape from town and unwind with my family after a busy work week.

As a kid, I was either taking off on my four-wheeler with a can of sardines in my pack, hunting for rattlesnakes with my mom or fishing for bass. I loved taking drives

My Unpacked Suitcase

with Dad to the mountains and listening to his stories. Together we would sing old country songs, shoot ground squirrels, and build things.

My closest brother taught me how to throw a punch. In third grade, I got called to the principal's office for bloodying my classmate's nose when he walked by our house on his way to school. I felt bad for Tony, but my brother had told me to tackle him, and not wanting to disappoint, I obeyed.

Early on, I learned how to back up a boat trailer and navigate the river. Small in stature, at the age of twelve, I stood about four feet eight. I got onlooker stares when my parents handed over the keys at the launch ramp, sending me to back the truck and trailer into the river to load the boat. It never dawned on me that I looked a little too small and shouldn't be doing that quite yet. I was spirited, and my brother, who taught me how to fight, also showed me how to use my middle finger when necessary. Flipping that bird landed me a spanking or two.

My freckles might have been cute when I was young. By adolescence, I resembled a short-haired, buck-toothed little boy more than a girl. In fact, one night at the local county fair, one of the "carnies" yelled out to my proud dad, "Hey mister, bring that handsome little fella up here and win him a stuffed animal." Dad promptly corrected the "carny" and we went home. The next morning as soon as we woke, he took me straight to our local jewelry store to get my ears pierced.

Being a hairdresser's daughter, I was often a guinea pig for the latest styles and trends when Mom came home from her hair shows. I sported baby bangs, mall bangs, and even a short wedge with an eight-inch tail colored half-pink and half-blue. Kinky perms and good ol' bobs: I wore them all with pride. The kids at school thought I looked cool, but their parents usually gave me an odd squint and head tilt.

Mom always said, "Rules were made to be broken." She told me I could do anything I wanted, so I thought so too.

I knew zero middle ground. I am either *all* in or *all* out. Halfway isn't something I know. This is a trait that has both helped and hindered me along my way.

One day in second grade, my best friend showed up at school in her pink leotard and headband and threw a standing back handspring. I knew in an instant that I wanted to learn that trick. Having a petite frame and a muscular build, I quickly took to the gymnastics world.

My Unpacked Suitcase

My coach was strict and required us to be fully dedicated. We worked out two and a half hours a night, four nights per week. We weren't allowed to chase boys or be involved in any other sport. We said a nightly pledge dedicating ourselves to our teammates and coaches. The sport taught me a great deal of coordination and discipline, and I developed lifelong friendships with many of my teammates.

I was a competitive gymnast, eventually gaining the gold-medal title of Idaho's all-around. I quietly battled terrible performance anxiety. They actually had to pause a few meets so I could run to the bathroom with my nervous tummy. The only thing I feared more than performing in front of a crowd was letting down my parents and coaches. Eight years later after two serious injuries, our doctor decided it was time for something new, and my career as a gymnast was done. I was secretly relieved!

My entire life, I was always a tomboy. Aside from a couple soul sisters who enjoyed Hells Canyon with me, I was more comfortable around boys than sitting around looking pretty with the girls, talking about our outfits. I don't easily open up about my feelings. I'd much rather learn about you and hold my stuff inside. It took me many years to figure out how heavy this can be. I can go for a hike and process things or throw myself into "work mode" to keep it locked up for a while. But eventually we have to talk about stuff.

We did not attend church unless my Grandma Ann, Dad's mom, guilted us into going with her to the Assemblies of God church. She was the strongest Christian I knew. She loved her church and looked forward to attending a couple services each week. For so many like my grandma, church is a wonderful place to connect and be filled up with God's Word. She loved Jesus, and she loved to pray. She was very old-school; Grandma's laws required strict perfection in my young eyes, and they seemed too hard to live by.

After Grandma passed, I received her large-print Bible. I've come to regret not taking more time to talk with her about Jesus. She never held back her opinions about our sinful way of not going to church every Sunday. When we did go along with her, being there felt like some kind of punishment. After the preaching, I left feeling confused, guilty, and certain that I was going to hell.

While in junior high, one evening I went to the Valley Christian Church with a couple of friends for a teenage

My Unpacked Suitcase

gathering. In the middle of a song, a boy about sixteen years old dropped to the floor and began jerking about. I thought he was having a seizure. Everyone rushed to his side and began pointing and yelling at him. Evidently, he'd been playing with a Ouija board, and he had encountered some demons that were on their way out. He hissed like a snake and violently convulsed for several minutes. I was scared out of my mind, so I found the closest exit. My brother had convinced me that our house was haunted, so I knew a thing or two about ghosts. But I didn't understand this exorcism, and it was enough to make me uncomfortable in any church for a long time.

My prayers used to be sort of one-sided, with me asking for things. I had memorized a few old nursery rhymes for protection while I slept to keep nightmares at bay. I had been taught what was in the Bible, and I always had one easily accessible on my end table. But I wasn't comfortable opening it up and actually reading it. The wording seemed to go right over my head.

I love adventuring outdoors. To this day, I find it hard to be around town or crowds on the weekends. I pout a little if we don't get mountain or river time. It's where I find my peace, and I feel closer to God there than anywhere else. Since I'm not a "church fan," I've developed a relationship with God outside those four walls.

Beauty in Nature

Here in the Northwest, we live in an outdoorsman's dream. We are blessed with the Blue Mountains full of wildlife and wonder, caves and canyons. We have just enough snow to thrill our winter-loving adrenaline junkies who snowmobile and ski. We have elk, deer, bears, cougars, bobcats, snakes, pine trees, wildflowers, and bright orange skies. We also have the Snake River, and I'm lucky enough to have been raised in the heart of it.

At two weeks old, my parents bundled me up and we ventured into Hells Canyon to our little cabin. As I grew, we would load the boat and head up every weekend. In the summer on Wednesdays, my mom's day off, she would load me up and we would spend the day tanning, catching bass, and learning to run new river channels in Dad's boat. Sometimes we would have an easy trip and

Beauty In Nature

other times we would get a flat tire on the trailer or an occasional stick in the pump.

We fixed things with our makeshift tools. In Hells Canyon, there are no roads; it's accessible only by boat. When something breaks down, there is no store to run to for parts and no one to call for help. You make do with what you have on hand and fix it yourself.

The summer I was fourteen, my best girlfriend and I spent two weeks there. We towheaded girls had one adventure after another. Alone with no adult supervision, we swam, floated, fished, and met fellow river runners who became friends. We went in the moonlight to a natural hot spring a couple miles upstream with two old timers and listened to their stories all night long. We ran rapids, killed snakes, and slept under the stars on the deck. If a stranger showed up at our place, we greeted him armored in bikinis and a holstered pistol. We got a little drunk and lot sunburned.

Some of our very best stories come from those two weeks together in the canyon. When we tell our kids about it now, we shake our heads at our insane parents for allowing us to be on such an adventure without them. I thank God for letting me live here with this river. I thank

My Unpacked Suitcase

Him for that best girlfriend and our adventures together. Most of all, I thank Him for sending His river to help shape me, and for all the memories we've made on it. It is one of His many gifts in my life.

The Cabin

*This place where I go,
When the path I'm walking on seems a bit hazy,
there is this place where I go.
There is this place where I go, it's the very place
He goes, I know.
The crickets sing here and the birds are cheery.
It's where the river echoes and the water below
reflects what's above.
It's where the memories are only strong enough to
make me thankful of my time.
Oh, the pillows are musty and the sheets are sandy.
The dishes are plastic and the spiders are plenty.
But there is this place where I go,
Where the food always tastes better,
The air always cleaner,
The stars always brighter, and
Life just seems a bit sweeter.
Where I can look to the sky
And time doesn't matter.*

Beauty In Nature

*I know that lives are changed and dreams
can be shattered,
But plans are made and prayers are answered.
Today is mine and no one can take it. In spite of it all,
I'm going to live it!
Thank God for this place*

Let's Go Back, but Not Stay Long

After graduating high school, I took some business classes at a local community college. I got married and went on to follow my mom's footsteps at the salon. My husband at the time encouraged me to take the quickest path to a solid income. Any dreams I had of a career that required expensive schooling went out the door.

Let me take you back to that first marriage. I was nineteen, and he was twenty-four. He had goals and drive, and he was tight with his money. He was a huge list maker, and he was faithful. My heart was still broken and scarred from a long, rocky "first love" relationship in high school. Instead of taking time to regroup, I focused on trying to fix and rescue my first husband. He felt like a good choice, although he'd had a rough childhood and came with some demons of his own. I remember thinking to myself, *As long as he doesn't cheat on me, I can handle anything!* I thought if I showered him with enough love, I could somehow help him change.

This held true for a short time, but then we got too comfortable and quit trying to impress each other. We didn't put much effort into our relationship. He didn't like my family, and he didn't want me to spend time away from him. He needed all my attention, and I struggled with letting go of my close friendships. I had been mistaken in thinking I could still be young and have fun, while chasing my dreams and being married.

As time passed, our differences magnified, our disagreements escalated, and I found myself stuck. By then, I was twenty-five years old and I was looking out at life, feeling like I was trapped in a prison. In an attempt to make things better, we decided to have a baby, and we welcomed our son into the world.

Around this time, my parents' twenty-six-year marriage came to a screeching halt. They went through an ugly divorce of their own, and I felt their pain. I became counselor for both sides, trying to keep the peace. I felt sorry for my dad because he was left alone, while my mom married his lifelong best friend within the year.

There were so many rumors and fires to put out in our small town; it felt like everywhere we went, people were gossiping about my family and my life. Clients came in and wanted to talk about it. Old friends at the grocery store had questions. It felt like our lives were on display. I was not a little girl anymore, but even as an adult, I found it exhausting some days to keep my composure. But they were my parents, and because my mom was also my business partner, I had to ignore my personal feelings. I tried to focus on the fact that they both deserved happiness, even if they weren't together. I loved them greatly, and I wanted peace as quickly as possible.

My husband could see the toll this was taking on me. Out of fear and insecurity, he developed "rules" for me to follow. I had to stop visiting girlfriends after work, and infrequent purchases like a twelve-dollar blouse at Walmart were forbidden. He wanted to know why I was "wasting" money rather than staying focused on "our goals."

On my days off, along with being a mom, I often woke up to a list of things he wanted me to accomplish for the day placed by the coffee pot. A typical list included getting

Let's Go Back, But Not Stay Long

the oil changed in the boat, mowing the lawn, pulling weeds, cleaning the house, making him a special dinner, etc. Inside, I was crumbling.

As years passed, I began to despise our life. I grew older and found my own voice and backbone. I went from being a controllable girl who wanted to save him to being an independent woman who needed him to save himself. He hated the person I became, and quite frankly, I felt the same about him. I had lost myself in trying to be everything he needed. Instead of growing together, we completely fell apart.

One day while he was at work, I loaded our boat full of my and our son's clothes and drove out of the driveway of our beautiful new home on the golf course. I left him with his big house and money and was gone. Looking back, I wish I had handled things differently, but at the time, it was all I had the strength for.

Thankfully, time has healed our relationship, and we're now friends. I even cut his hair occasionally. I'm thankful for this relationship because he ended up being a great dad for our son.

Unfortunately, my thought process after this was along the lines of, *Okay, stupid, let's not take any time to heal.*

My Unpacked Suitcase

Let's jump right into another relationship and put a band aid on this pain. This brings me to marriage number two. Along came a confident, smooth-talking, friendly, funny, tattooed smartass who was the life of the party and also a giant life lesson for me. We had been good friends for years, so loving him came easy. He showered me with affection and attention.

He was an overgrown child in a man's body, a walking Disneyland. He claimed he was "blessed with immaturity." I agreed and laughed it off. It was like a breath of fresh air. When we got married, we promised each other, "When this is no longer fun, let's not do it."

We owned two Harleys, two four-wheelers, two snow-mobiles, and fancy new vehicles. We bought whatever we wanted, and we lived one good time after another. Eventually, I found out that you have to *pay* for Disneyland, and the bills came rolling in. Lines were crossed, trust was broken, and BOOM, the fun house came tumbling down. I now know that you can't build a marriage on good times without first giving it a foundation.

At first I thought it was the time of my life. I felt like I was living life to the fullest! We had good times for nearly ten years. Business was good; I opened a second salon location, which required an exhausting seventy-hour work week.

My dad suffered a heart attack and had to have quadruple bypass surgery. My mom had financial troubles. My friends had their struggles. My son, my coworkers, and my husband all needed my time and energy. I threw on my imaginary cape and saved the day, rescuing them with one life raft after another. Being a mom, wife, daughter, friend, and now a boss of two locations, I gave every effort to hold everyone up. I put on a big ol' smile and became the best rescuer I could be. I felt like I was swimming as hard as possible, but I could no longer hold my head above the water. I was drowning!

I recalled that stupid, naive promise my second husband and I had made years earlier. At this point, things were no longer "fun," and I couldn't keep up. I found myself empty, scared, and alone in the middle of a crowd. I was lost, financially broke, brokenhearted, devoid of peace, and emotionally devastated.

Looking back, I believe I was in that season for a definite purpose as a part of God's plan for the bigger picture of my life. Romans 8:18 says, "I consider that our present sufferings are not worth comparing with the glory that will be revealed in us."

During that second marriage, I gained an unlikely best friend: his ex-wife. I was also fortunate to become a stepmother to an incredible "bonus" daughter. During these years, I started relationships with some of the greatest people I know. I'm still thankful for that period of my life. It showed me more about who I am and who I am *not* than any other time of my life. It brought me to a time of "quietness and desperation" that I had never known. It knocked the wind out of me and dropped me to my knees. Isaiah 41:13 says, "For I am the Lord your God who takes hold of your right hand and says to you Do not fear; I will help you."

When that second marriage was over, I knew I needed to regroup. I could see a pattern in my life that was not serving me well. I made myself a promise to heal old wounds and fix what was broken inside of me. I was determined not to fall into the same patterns. I needed to figure out how to take care of myself first. I spent a lot of time on walks and went on a faith-based self-help reading crusade while enjoying many talks with God. I read my Bible because I needed to learn for myself what was in it.

I am a natural-born fighter. Even though I was filled with deep sadness about my second failed marriage, I gained a new sense of awareness I hadn't known in my past. When the storm was over, I came out with a new sense of who I was. The question, "Lord, why?" ended up bringing me to a place of great joy and hope. Isaiah 43:2–3 says, "When you pass through the waters, I will be with you; and when you pass through the rivers, they will not sweep over you. When you walk through the fire, you will not be burned; the flames will not set you ablaze. For I am the Lord your God, the Holy One of Israel, your Savior."

I took time to get to know the "me" I always wanted to be. I gained a new sense of purpose and strongly felt that the Lord was shaping me for something better. It took me being down and lost to get me to look up for help and lean on a greater power than myself. I had to hand it all over because the fun-spirited, always-smiling superwoman was holding everyone up but herself. I was carrying a heavy load of crap on my shoulders before I took off my pack and gave it up. When I did, I know God smiled and said, *"Finally!* I've got you. Now let's dance!"

Time for a Bath

When my son was five years old, while sitting in the bathtub one day, he looked up at me with his big blue eyes and said, "Mom, why did you and my dad get a divorce?"

It was a serious question that carried the weight of a lot of grown-up junk. When I looked at those eyes, I knew this was a big moment. I needed to be as gentle but honest as possible. I took a deep breath, looked him square in the eye, and began. "Well, Kaegen, you know your daddy and me. Now, are we the same at all?"

"No way," he said.

On I continued. "Sometimes when people are so different from each other, it's kind of hard to live in the same house. By different, I don't mean *bad*. It's just that we are not the same. And that's *okay*. It's easier if we live in

Time For A Bath

separate homes. We can still love you and be good parents even if we don't live under one roof."

"Well," he said, serious as could be, "I just can't decide who I love the most."

In my small bathroom, the air got heavy. I was ashamed that my little guy felt he had to carry my load. "Well, Kaegen," I replied, "you see, that's the thing about love. You have an endless supply in your heart. You don't have to choose, because *love* has no end. You can love your dad the most, your grandma and papa the most, and me the most. You don't ever have to choose, because we are all different. The love you have will be different for each one of us."

I knew from his big ol' sigh of relief that the weight of *our* junk that our five-year-old was carrying had eased a bit.

As his mom, it's my job to protect him at all costs. By "protect" him, I don't mean just keeping him safe. I need to protect him on the inside as well as the outside. I needed to deliver him from carrying my suitcase of crap around with him, because I knew he was going to grow, have experiences of his own, and have his own suitcase to carry. If I did my job well, I would show him how to ask God to unpack that baggage and walk free from his junk as well.

His dad and I had our share of ugliness for many years, with restraining orders and messy divorce dealings, but my son's heavy question in the tub that day was enough to keep me in check. He continued to grow, I remained positive, and he never heard me bad-mouth his dad. Although I know my son has felt the tension, he has never had to choose between us. Thank you, God, for loving him and protecting him from my garbage, and thank you for giving me the wisdom to see that my son deserves to grow in a peaceful environment.

Today, many years later, I've remarried a third time (I'll explain later) and I'm blessed with a couple more incredible bonus daughters. Being a stepmom (or "bonus" mom, as I like to call it) comes with its own set of challenges. There have been moments when I've had to remind myself of my own saying: "Remember, LynnDee, there is enough love, even for a bonus mom." Stepparenting by balancing love and support without stepping on their mom's toes is a challenge. After all, they already have a mom, and I respect that. I've learned that my place is to support their parents and have a positive impact on them as they grow. I try to free them from the weight of carrying adult problems and give them the peace of mind that they too never have to choose between us.

As parents, we seem to automatically want a flawless life for our children. Yet when we look at our own lives, we see that our bumps in the road and hard times led us to strength and showed us what we were really made of. Romans 5:3–4 says, "Not only so but we rejoice in our sufferings, because we know that suffering produces perseverance; perseverance, character; and character, hope."

Social media tends to portray perfect families with perfect lives. But with a perfect life, we'd have no inner strength or determination. We'd have no stories to share, and we certainly wouldn't need Jesus. Instead of faking perfection, let's teach our kids how to deal with life. Let's give them tools to survive their own storms, and let's help them know where to turn when they need to be saved.

Not Just a Leaf

We have to take time to clean our internal closet. Cleaning out our junk keeps us from unnecessarily placing blame on others and helps us not pass it on to our children. Sometimes during the cleaning, we gain perspective on why something may have happened or why we behaved a certain way. A friend of mine once told me, "When you know better, you do better." That simple phrase sent me on a voyage of discovery to "know better" about myself and to cut myself some grace for not "knowing better" in the past.

We might suffer only to learn a lesson of forgiveness. Sometimes we suffer consequences of bad decisions in order to grow into better people in the future. Sometimes there seems to be no rhyme or reason to our suffering. Maybe it's not up to us to have all the answers when we want them. Sometimes our story helps set someone else free.

Life has a way of dealing us cards that seem unfair and undeserved. Young children get put in bad situations, and adults suffer great losses. Teenagers get abused and bullied through social media. Sometimes we are the one at fault, and sometimes we aren't.

By reflecting on my own experiences and observing others in my life, I've found that if we don't take the time to free ourselves from the burden of pain or guilt, we get stuck in a repetitive cycle of nonsense that we can't find our way out of. Allow yourself to feel it. Then deal with it, sending it away once and for all. Write about it and burn the letter up if you have to. Either way, be done hurting about it. If we don't do this, it's like we get dressed from the dirty clothes hamper every day. No matter how nice we look, we're still going to stink.

Satan loves to keep us paralyzed in our past, bringing up our failures and mistakes time after time. He loves to remind us of our insecurities and to keep our minds preoccupied with the chaos of pain. Once the junk from our internal closet is gone, we find room for God. Then we have power to tell Satan we are not interested in his lies.

Don't be afraid to address parts of your life that need adjustment. It's never too late to reshape our behavior. Prayer, studying the Bible, and looking within are vitally important for awareness of how your spirit is handling "life." When you start to feel bogged down, short-tempered, and like you're packing a heavy load, hand it over, forgive, and release.

Several such moments helped change me, but one day stands out. I was walking along the river, feeling like I was carrying the weight of the entire world on my shoulders. I stood there, crying and trying to process my life. It was a particularly tough time for me. I wasn't sure where things were headed or if I was ever going to feel true happiness again. I was struggling with the pain of my broken marriages and friendships, guilt for causing pain to people I cared about, and the shame of being a complete failure in many areas of my life.

I sat down and noticed a pretty little leaf lying on the ground beside me. It was bright orange and shaped like a heart. I picked it up and held on to it, surprised by its beauty. I watched the river pass by, carrying sticks and leaves away in its current. I was mesmerized by the beauty in front of me, which changed with each second.

Just as one thing would disappear out of my sight, something new would appear.

For some reason, I held that leaf up to my mouth and did something strange. I started blowing into it. I blew rotten air from deep inside me that was full of regrets, shame, and heartache. I blew and I blew and I blew. Then I placed the leaf into the water and watched as the current took it away. Gone! I let it go!

I sat there feeling relieved and light. I felt the breeze blow in my hair, and I heard the birds chirping all around me. I went from sobbing to laughing at how silly I must look, sitting there blowing my life into a leaf. But that moment was a game changer. I stood up and walked away a little different from the inside out.

Ephesians 4:31–32 says, "Get rid of all bitterness, rage and anger, brawling and slander, along with every form of malice. Be kind and compassionate to one another, forgiving each other, just as in Christ God forgave you." Rivers change things. The water flows over sharp rocks and they become round. I took a lesson from the river, learning to allow God's river to flow over and reshape me. Grow me! Make me better, Lord, because without You, I feel lost.

A New Start

When I finally started a routine of listening to and leaning on the Lord, our relationship grew stronger. He shows me so much beauty in nature, which is a gift from above. I've learned to count on Him for strength and guidance. I am finally surviving, and even more than that, I am living a life I love from the inside out. I read, write, walk, listen, learn, and grow. Isaiah 40:31 says, "But those who hope in the Lord will renew their strength. They will soar on wings like eagles; they will run and not grow weary; they will walk and not be faint."

I used to begin from the second my feet hit the floor. I would get up, make my family a warm breakfast, go for a hike, get the kids off to school, glance at the newspaper, clean up the house, take a shower, do my hair and face, get dressed, run into my home office to pay bills, and race to the salon. Cut, rinse, and dry one customer after

A New Start

the next. I would run back home for a break, set something out for dinner. Speed over town for salon supplies, crunch numbers for employees, then head back behind the chair to bleach, weave, scrub, and smile, giving excellent customer service. Dazzle here, juggle there, starving, shovel in a spoonful of peanut butter, and back at it. My responses always had a friendly tone: "Yes, I can fit you in." "Yes, it's okay that you're late." "Yes, I see you cut your own bangs." I'd glance at the clock, see that it was 8 p.m., race home, and kick off my heels. I'd be happy to see my family, just in time to help with homework or a science project. My reply was always, "I got it." Finally, it was time for sleep, I'd collapse and then I'd do it all over again the next day.

    I had this crazy idea that rest was for the old or sick, not me. During a helpful conversation with my Savior, He showed me that it was okay to take a break, refuel and rest. That didn't mean I was lazy. No, quite the opposite; it actually made me better. When Satan can't make you bad, he makes you too busy. But Psalm 46:10 says, "Be still, and know that I am God."

    I began to own my day instead of it owning me. I sold my second location and cut back on work hours. I allowed the people in my life to help me, and I found that they had wanted to all along. While I was busy taking care of everything on my own, I was actually taking away opportunities for them to give me their gifts. We show love through our actions. By letting them step in and show me a little love, we began to work as a well-oiled machine.

My coworkers began to flourish and grow, and I took deep breaths and figured out how to be present with each person, rather than worrying about my next task. I have mountains of appreciation for the people who stepped up. *Good-bye fog, hello clarity!* There wasn't much peace or calm in my past life, but through prayer and growth, I've become filled with it. By stepping back and assessing my own life instead of pointing the finger at others, I was able to rest and allow God's light to shine through me. He healed me and gave me so much joy. There is such a sense of fulfillment in letting God guide you rather than running around on empty by yourself. There is much greater peace in being present.

When your friends say, "You've changed," own it. Take a deep breath and smile, because it isn't easy to clean out your closet. It takes work, it takes facing ugly truths, and it takes realizing that your story's not over. *Give it a try and thrive.* When it gets hard, look up. When it gets easier, still look up. When the sun rises, look up. When you see His work and signs each day, look up and say, "I know that was You, God. Thank you!"

Now third time is a charm and I'm happily married to my soul mate, Shawn, and we started our life together with an abundance of love. It's the first time I've loved someone for *me* rather trying to fix them or be their life raft, and it's not a relationship based on what the last one lacked. It took me more tries than most, but I finally got it right.

My husband is my best friend and my steady hand to hold as we share good days and bad. I know without a shadow of doubt that he will always have my back. I catch myself staring at him in awe that God loved me enough to bless me with this man. He is an introverted, gentle soul who carries a strength inside that my soul requires. He manages to balance me in all my ways.

Our marriage was put into God's capable hands right from the start. It came with the commitment of forever and the strength to make it happen. When I look at my past, I appreciate those broken pieces and forks in the road. Without my failures, I might not appreciate where I am now.

We vowed "for better or for worse" at our cabin in Hells Canyon, surrounded by our friends and family. It was a day full of promises, not only to each other but to our kids and family. The day was filled with God's promises all around us. First Corinthians says, "Now these three remain: faith, hope and love. But the greatest of these is love" (13:13), and "Love is patient, love is kind. It does not envy, it does not boast, is not proud. It does not dishonor others, it is not self-seeking, it is not easily angered, it keeps no record of wrongs" (13:4).

I've learned to be a better wife and partner through my walk with God. I've started a couple new routines. I wake up early in the morning before work and begin each day with my Savior. We talk about the day, and I lay my worries and fears at His feet. I ask for the courage to be brave in His name. In these morning conversations, I have total peace that together we can face whatever comes along. I've found that if I don't have this meeting with Him, I feel like I'm stepping out the door with only one shoe. I feel less prepared, walking in circles, less strong and clear.

A New Start

Two mornings a week, I take appointments at the salon at 5 a.m. This means I have to wake up at 3 a.m. in order to have private time with God. Even though it means I need a nap in the afternoon, it is well worth the effort to start my day out right.

I'm not saying God's going to make you perfect or turn you into something you're not. He won't take away your feisty, adventurous spirit. We're human. If you're anything like me, you'll probably still say a swear word or two, battle anxiety, drive too fast, love to skinny dip, and have a bit of a dirty mind. You'll still have bad days, and confusion will arise, but when it does, you now have superpowers to help you cope and peace knowing that God is at your side.

We won't get everything right, but when we screw up, we have His amazing grace. In Luke 7:50, "Jesus said to the woman, 'Your faith has saved you; go in peace.'" He shows us our God-given gifts and helps us do His work. He fills us with more love than we can ever imagine. He's been there all along, protecting, providing, helping, growing, and watching over us. He wants to help us find our true identity in Him and to enjoy the gifts in our life. When we walk with and seek Him, He will provide a freedom, we have never known but always longed for. Exodus 14:14 says, "The Lord will fight for you; you need only to be still," and John 14:18 says, "I will not leave you as orphans; I will come to you."

In the Low Times, We Find Our Answers

One day, life happened and I landed at an unfamiliar place, knocked quiet by bad news. A friend my son snowmobiled with was killed by an avalanche. This followed another accident where a lifelong family friend's son was injured, hit on the head by falling debris while driving a tractor on their mountain property. He was in a coma for more than a month, and the odds were he would not survive. Thank God he did, but his recovery and rehabilitation have been grueling.

The two accidents were the first real life-and-death pain my son had to face at the young age of eighteen. This was the first time in his life that I was unable to "fix it." Watching him struggle with life's questions literally knocked the wind out of me. One Monday morning, I was off work and silent. In search of some help, I reached for my Bible. I prayed a mother's plea: "Lord, please help me. I don't know what to do." Saying one prayer after another, I spent most of the day reading and talking to God, brought to Him on my knees. I opened up and apologized for my faults and failures, listing all the rotten things I'd been hiding due to shame and guilt. Nothing spectacular happened; it was just a heavyhearted day during which I spent time with God and searched for answers.

I believe He had been waiting for me to get to that place, but I had been consumed with life. I know that He's waiting to do the same things for you! He wants you to empty yourself of the things that are not filling you up: vices, booze, social media, work, negative thoughts, unhealthy relationships, guilt, shame, betrayal, and pain. He is able to take them from you and fill you up with an absurd amount of His goodness.

On Tuesday morning when I awoke, I felt lighter and had a better sense that things were going to be okay. I saw my son before school, and I noticed that his eyes seemed a little less weary. After a good-bye hug, he was off to tackle Tuesday.

That morning while blow-drying my hair, I was struck with a jolt from the Holy Spirit. I couldn't hear, see, or touch it, yet it felt like I could do all three at once. It was as though I was vibrating from deep inside my soul. I laid the blow-dryer down and held on to the counter to steady myself. I could see my life unfolding, watching my failures and successes at once, but separately and clearly. I couldn't audibly hear voices, but I could understand them. I saw visions. I could feel the pain of two failed marriages, and I received the answers to questions I'd been wondering, including why I'd become a hair stylist twenty years previously.

In the vision, I saw a circle of light drawn by the hand of God. My past, present and future all came together and made total sense in my heart. I stood in a trance, staring at the ground. Then I heard—or more like *felt*—Him say, "Hey, little one, I made you brave and bold on purpose. I've got something I want you to do for Me. It's time to gather your people and begin."

At that moment, I knew I had been given the answers I'd been desperately searching for the day before. I knew what I was supposed to do, and I knew that He would be right beside me, guiding me and giving me the courage to have awkward conversations. I felt a fire begin to burn inside me.

My Unpacked Suitcase

I sped to work that morning, thankful that my car had a speakerphone. All lit up from the inside out, I took off at full throttle. I had places to go and people to call that day!

She Believed She Could So She Did

I used to second-guess my career choice, but I know I was placed there to observe and learn about people. In the salon industry, when a client sits in our chair beneath the security of the cape, they open up and share things about themselves that they wouldn't normally talk about. I believe that God brings us who we need when we need them. I now look at my place of business as an opportunity to touch people, both inside and out. "Blessed is she who has believed that the Lord would fulfill his promises to her" (Luke 1:45).

One by one, I approached my coworkers and close friends with the idea of starting a Bible study. This is what I heard from them: "I've been needing something like this." "I've been a little lost." "I've been headed down the wrong path." "I don't know what to believe." "I don't know anything about the Bible, but my life is missing something." "I'm stupid when it comes to God." "I've never opened my Bible." "I know nothing about religion." With each conversation, seeing the tears in their eyes, I knew I was on the right track. The date was set and it was time for me to do my homework.

I knew I needed to give them something different, a place other than the church, which they were uncomfortable with. So, we chose to close early on Wednesday evenings at the salon and meet there. It was a place where we could feel safe and at ease to open up, where it was okay to be ourselves. A place of freedom, hope, and love. A place to be women, wives, daughters, and moms searching for our place in this world.

I gathered information from different clients about Bible studies and shared with a trusted few what I was planning. Then along came Deborah. She was one of my longest-running, most loyal clients, and she suggested Angie Smith's *Seamless* study. Now I had the right study. I began taking notes on what I thought I should talk about. Page by page, I wrote a direction for our *Seamless* group and points I wanted to share with them. I kept in close contact with God because Satan was whispering words of doubt and negativity, causing me fear and anxiety. I had moments where I felt totally off my rocker, followed by moments of knowing I was doing exactly what I was called to do.

Trying to plan a gathering for God brought a lot of pressure. Driving to the first study with my pile of materials and butterflies thick in my gut, I thought I was going to poop my pants. With the stereo off, all I could do was pray. "Lord," I said, "please help them show up. Please help me not to freak out and freeze up. Please guide me, because we both know I can't do this thing on my own."

There are great words in Scripture about turning our anxiety over to Him. Psalm 138:3 says, "When I called, you answered me; you greatly emboldened me." First Peter 5:7 says, "Cast all your anxiety on him because he cares for you." And Philippians 4:5–6 says, "Let your gentleness be evident to all. The Lord is near. Do not be anxious about anything, but in every situation, by prayer and petition, with thanksgiving, present your requests to God."

That night, we had a whopping twenty-two ladies in attendance. Matthew 18:20 says, "For where two or three gather in my name, there am I with them," and Proverbs 27:17 says, "As iron sharpens iron, so one person sharpens another."

My Unpacked Suitcase

In the past, parties have not been my thing. One on one at my station, I'm completely comfortable, but put me in a group of people making awkward small talk and I'll hide in the corner, looking for the closest exit. I've been known to host parties where no one showed up because I didn't actually invite anyone, including Bunco, Mary Kay, Tupperware, and "pleasure" parties. I've had some embarrassing moments trying to explain to the rep why no one showed up. It usually costs me an arm and a leg because I order more than I need to make up for the lack of attendance. Not this time, though. They all showed up!

With a packed house and no place to sit, I took one last deep breath and walked right into the middle of the group. I boldly sat down cross-legged on the floor in front of them and began speaking. The Lord showed up that night and helped me deliver the message He wanted. It may have been my mouth speaking, but the stuff coming from it was not what I was used to.

There were stories, tears, and laughter. We were a group of misfit ladies learning about the Lord and growing in ways we had never imagined. We were brought together on purpose for His purpose. When the night was over, I glanced over at the pile of papers beside me and realized I had never once looked at them.

Each time we meet, I am amazed at what God is doing within our group. On some nights we have a packed house, and on others we are a small group. But I have come to trust that the people who were meant to hear the message of the evening will be present. It works out every time, one "God moment" after another.

When the study was over for that season, I invited the group to join me on a beach along the beautiful Snake River in late June to do baptisms. On that magical evening, fifteen people showed up, took off their old skin, and were born again in the name of our heavenly Father. Romans 10:9 says, "If you declare with your mouth, 'Jesus is Lord,' and believe in your heart that God raised him from the dead, you will be saved." That night, I was a witness to something much bigger than myself. Words cannot describe the emotions and healing that poured from us that night. Thank you, God, for making it happen in that way and at that time.

They say there are no chance encounters, and that each person in your life was brought there for a reason. Our group feels magical together.

My Unpacked Suitcase

Being a Christian doesn't have to be reserved for Sundays inside a church building. It isn't just for seemingly well-put-together people. It's for *all* of us. It's for the mistake-making purple-haired, pierced, tattooed children of God. It's for the wrecked, the lost, the confused, and the broken. It's for the stubborn, the free-spirited, the adventure-seeking, and the foot-stomping. It's for *you* and *me*.

Having a relationship with God doesn't mean judgment and hypocrites or man-made rules and regulations. A relationship deep inside our hearts and souls, which crave to be filled up with His abundant love. Our relationship with Him is not about having all the answers or being able to pronounce all the names in the Bible. It's about trusting, listening, obeying, and keeping faith when everything else seems uncertain. It's a real relationship with Jesus every day of the week.

Some Things Are Worth Remembering, While Some Are Worth Ignoring

I attended a salon conference out of state years ago held by Peter Mahoney, one of the greatest speakers I've ever heard. When he said, "Repeat this phrase because it will end up being important," I sat up and paid attention. He then stated, *"Your opinion is none of my business!"*

There have been plenty of times when I've been tied up in worry about others' opinions. In reality, this simple, silly phrase makes a lot of sense. We are all unique, and there will be people who aren't wired the same as you, and therefore, won't like you. That's *okay*. I've learned that I don't need to spend sleepless nights worrying about it. Typically, they are struggling with pain we know nothing about. Praying for them is the most powerful way to give them a hand. The Bible doesn't say we have to fix them or convince them to see things the way we do. We just have to *love* them.

If you are loving, living, praying, and thriving, you won't have room for negativity. The less value we place on the opinions of people who aren't meant for us, the more time we have to enjoy the people who do love and need us. I've wasted so many days worrying about things that weren't for me. My mom told me years ago, "Never give someone enough power to ruin your perfectly good day." It took me a long time to figure that one out, but it finally stuck.

Our time on earth is short, and I don't want to waste it with worry, rumors, bad attitudes, and negative social media comments that fuel Satan's fire. He loves it when we're filled with chaos and confusion. Those are his weapons. But when we stand with God, we have the power to disarm him. Ephesians 6:11 says, "Put on the full armor of God, so that when the day of evil comes, you may be able to stand your ground."

Everywhere we go, most of us are on our phones, scanning through social media. I've met people who admittedly spend five hours a day scrolling. *Stop the insanity!* If it's not filling us with peace, and if it's causing anxiety or jealousy by making us compare our life to others, then quit looking at it. If that's where we find ourselves, let's take a look at how it's affecting our lives.

Are we stuck on the toilet for thirty minutes, scrolling or feverishly looking at someone's pictures when their life is none of our business? Are we feeding into their nonsense, or are we living our life to its fullest? I can almost guarantee that when God made us, He didn't say, "Now, this one here is going to grow up to be a tremendous Facebook queen. I'll give her better fingers so she can easily scroll."

It's not that social media can't be used in a positive way; I'm just suggesting that we should be aware of how we spend our time. Are you looking into the eyes of your kids, reading them stories? Are you going to lunch with a friend or helping your neighbor? When was the last time you made your husband feel special? Have we become a society of mindless wanderers going along with the rest of the world in Zombieland?

If we have, let's put our foot down and give it up. Let's want more from life. Set your phone down or put it on silent. Step outside and smell the fresh air. The Lord gives

My Unpacked Suitcase

us beautiful days. What a gift! Go for a walk and notice God's handiwork. Surprise your family with a homemade meal. Go "old-school" and actually converse or play a board game tonight. We need connections with the special people in our lives. Reach out and touch someone. I have a feeling you'll be so glad if you do!

My Perspective from Behind the Chair

*H*ave you ever laid in bed unable to sleep, with words swirling around inside your head? Just when you start to doze off, they pop back up, and you find yourself having a silent argument about how much you need to sleep. With the words nagging you and seeming important, you finally relinquish and stumble out of bed to find a pen to write them down.

I believe God sometimes comes to us at night when we are still and gives us answers to things we've been battling. Several years ago during a rough patch, I suddenly woke up in the middle of the night with something to say, I grabbed my laptop, and began writing. The following words poured out as fast as I could type.......

Who in their right mind listens to the little voices in their head? I guess I do. They say, "Who am I? Who are you? Is this my life? Is this the right path? Is this all there is? Because if that's the case, I want more!"

For twenty-plus years, I've stood behind the chair, talking to people while making their hair beautiful. We talk about their kids, husbands, lovers, parents, grandparents, best friends, enemies, divorces, weight, diet, and sleep patterns. They tell their stories, and we discuss what they should have done, what they want to do, where they went to school, where they shop, and what they like—and sometimes we even talk about their hair.

I have heard it all. I truly believe that most of them come back to me because I can offer small pieces of advice to help them, or because I at least entertain them. I've also found that most people don't necessarily want me to tell them what to do. A lot of them have all the answers they need; they just want someone to listen to them to sort it all out. When I was younger, I offered up more of my opinion. These days, I prefer to listen and ask questions. I have learned a lot about their lives, but when it's all said and done, I believe I have learned even more about myself and who I am from these conversations.

From them I have learned that the pretty ones are insecure about trivial things. Every overweight person

My Perspective From Behind The Chair

wants to be skinny, and every thin person wants to be thinner. No one "likes drama," but the people who proclaim to hate it the most are usually the ones causing it. I've learned that the poor usually tip more than the rich. Parents think their kids are perfect, no matter how old they are. Men like to talk about sex. Women like to talk about sex.

No one likes to lose. Everyone intends to volunteer, but only a small portion of us actually do it. Everyone wants to eat better. We all complain about how commercialized Christmas has become, yet we still buy things we don't need. Everyone has a funny story about poop. Most people say they are broke. Everyone is way too busy. Breakups trigger normal-functioning adults to act like emotional idiots. Most people get so caught up in what their ex is doing or not doing that they forget to protect their children from their own mess. Most of us blame someone else for our own issues. Good people sometimes do bad things. No one admits to spending time at the casino or surfing porn. Electronic gadgets have turned most of us into social idiots. Most people hate their cell phones but are always on them. A lot of people are miserable when they go home, but very few actually do anything to change this.

People spend a lot of time in front of my mirror, staring at themselves, but very few look and see what is right in front of them. Most of us are so caught up in our own routines and habits that we forget to take the time to pause and realize that we are not in control.

I have found that happy, optimistic people tend to be happy, no matter what is going on around them. The same applies for the down-in-the-dumps, gloom-and-doom types. They could be handed the world on a silver platter and still find a reason to complain. (For the record, I try to not work with these people because no matter what I do, their hair always looks "awful.")

True, authentic happiness isn't just a state-of-mind, it's a way of being. We can spot someone at peace from a mile away. It's in their walk, their facial expressions, and the aura of truth that exudes from them without saying a word. These people don't have perfect lives. What they do have is total peace and confidence in who they are and in the life they are living. They are honest, and they don't fret about the judgments of others. They are strong and independent. They know exactly what they want, and

My Perspective From Behind The Chair

they aren't afraid to have it. They are the ones we want to be around. We are drawn to them by an invisible force. We know we like them right from the start, we just don't usually know why. They carry a secret key to life that most of us try to find in all the wrong places. I'm not saying you have to know the Bible inside and out. But in the bad times, the horrible rip-your-heart-out, buckle-your-knees times, you need to know where to turn to for your courage.

I am far from perfect, I've been known to cuss like a sailor. I've been divorced twice and married three times. I enjoy a good drink and good lovin', and I can drive like a maniac. I love the summer sun, and I don't wear sunscreen. I enjoy being naked, and I rarely wash my hair. How is it that someone with these habits thinks that she would even deserve to ask the good Lord for assistance during the hardest times in her life? It's because I hold the key as well: *Jesus!*

If you want to stop sweating the small stuff, feeling like you're lost, and living an unfulfilled life, drop to your knees, dig down deep, take ownership of your actions, and start praying. When you are able to build from the inside out, you find out what you are made of and you become the person you were meant to be. It's really quite simple. Ask for forgiveness, ask for help, ask for strength, ask for answers, ask for health, ask for a friend, ask for peace, ask for anything you want—just look up and ask.

A lot of us are under the impression that we have to go to church to find the Lord. The truth is that He, God, the Creator of heaven and earth, is the Creator of *you*. When you need Him, He is not just inside the walls of a church. He is everywhere! He's in your car, in your house, in the mountains, and on the river. He is right beside you when you need Him the most. When you feel too stupid to ask Him for help because you've made an utter disaster of the life He gave you, He knows that too. So, you can quit hiding!

A feeling swept over me like I had completed my task. I closed my laptop and fell peacefully back to sleep!

Bread Crumbs

I love a good book or song that stirs something inside of me, and I've been blessed with a few that really stand out, helping to reshape who I was to who I am. I believe that God gives us little bread crumbs along our paths. When we pick them up and soak them in, we grow spiritually and we get closer to finding our true purpose.

I tend to be drawn to books that promote growth. I love to learn new ways to be better. *The Shack* by Wm. Paul Young gave me a new perspective on what a relationship with Jesus can look like. *The Resolution for Women* by Priscilla Shirer helped me take a look at myself and personally assess the kind of woman and wife I needed to be according to the Bible. *Looking for Lovely* by Annie F. Downs showed me how to notice God's amazing gifts that surround us all the time.

My Unpacked Suitcase

The *Seamless* study by Angie Smith was our first Bible study. Twenty-two ladies attended the study at my salon on Wednesday nights. This was an excellent place to learn about the stories inside our Bibles. We completed a workbook and watched her video. Angie Smith had a way of keeping it simple and real with modern-day words that helped us relate. She took the intimidation factor out and allowed us to openly discuss what we were feeling.

Our next study was *The End of Me* by Kyle Idleman. We decided to meet at my home for a more intimate setting and less interruptions. My house is quite small, so our group wasn't quite as large, but we were much more comfortable opening up. It was incredible to watch sixteen of us, cozied up in my living room, become brave and share our thoughts and fears. Kyle Idleman helped us develop a closer relationship with God by getting to the end of ourselves and finally looking up for our answers. A video also came with this study. The stories he shared were relatable, and they brought us to tears many times. We had to keep the box of Kleenex handy. This would be an excellent choice for both men's and women's groups.

Devotions for Christmas by Stacy Edwards helped Christmas feel magical again. As adults, we lose our childlike love for the season. It becomes so much work for us to make it special for our families. We cook meals, clean, and shop until we're exhausted, and we miss the delight we had when we were young. This little book is such a gift to me in December. Find it and fall in love with Christmas once again!

My all-time favorite is *Battlefield of the Mind* (book and study) by Joyce Meyer. I was intimidated by her work until this book was recommended to me by a good friend. As I sat and read through her pages, I loved her ability to show me that the battles inside my head served no purpose in my life. The book helped me evaluate my negative thoughts and patterns of fear and anxiety, and it gave me the tools to put an end to the nonsense once and for all.

I saved the best for last: the Bible. It's my go-to for direction and answers. If you have a Bible that intimidates you, please treat yourself to a new one. Invest in a cover that delights you when you look at it. I know the pages are thin and delicate, and the words can seem hard to understand, but not all Bibles are hard to follow. I know there is one out there that will suit your needs. When you find it, it will become your cherished treasure.

There are many other wonderful books out there, and I feel that we are handed the ones meant for us when the time is right.

Music also has a way of lighting us up. When I'm driving and listening to my "message" radio or cooking with Pandora blaring, my day is instantly brightened. I love to sing (especially when I'm alone in my car). A few songs have struck me and opened me up to messages I might have otherwise missed. "If We're Honest" and "Where Were You" by Francesca Battistelli are two such songs. She has a way of putting messages from my heart into words. She is my go-to when I need a lift.

"Still" by Hillary Scott reminds me of a message that God has sent me many times: "Be still, little one, I've got this." I smile and take a big sigh of relief knowing that He is in total control.

"Start a Fire" by Unspoken gets my hips shaking and my feet moving. I love to dance in the kitchen while I cook.

Shania Twain's "Today Is Your Day" gives me a positive boost in the morning when I feel too tired to tackle the long day.

"Blessings" by Laura Story helped me to see my blessings in the middle of my storms and disappointments.

Bread Crumbs

Some days when my world seems chaotic, I take a little pause to sit and be filled up by the music.

He Shows Up

When you are paying attention, you'll notice that you are given messages and little whispers throughout the day. I find when I am struggling with anxiety that if I can touch the cross I wear around my neck, I am instantly settled.

I put a little quote at my station at the salon to share with my guests: "She believed she could so she did." It's a simple reminder for me to hold tight to God's promises and believe in miracles. I see His work in my life every time someone sits down and mentions that quote.

One of my favorite stories from behind my chair is of a lady who was extremely worried about trying a new stylist. She had done her research and found out about my experience and techniques on line. When she came in, we were total strangers.

He Shows Up

As I cut her hair, I could feel pain exuding from inside her. When I was finished with her style, she glanced up, noticed that quote, and began to cry. I softly put my hands on her shoulders and asked if she needed to talk. Apparently, she had just found out that her brother was about to pass, and she shared with me about their tormented history. As she spoke, I silently prayed to find the right words for her. I happened to have a gap in my schedule that allowed us to visit for quite some time. Before she left, she wrapped her arms around me and said she knew that God had sent her to my chair. She told me that I gave her much more than just a haircut.

My eyes water a little when I tell that story because I know that God showed up once again for both of us. When He shows up in that way, I am humbled and grateful. I know that the words I gave her were what He wanted her to hear and what she needed for the strength and peace to get through this sad time.

If He is using this formerly lost and confused hairdresser living in a small part of the world to spread His good news, He will use you too! I hope that my story helps you dig down deep and set yourself free to live in the bright light of God's love. I might appear to be the

My Unpacked Suitcase

same ol' person on the outside, but from the depths of my soul, I am completely changed. I am finally settled and at total peace. My heavy suitcase is unpacked, emptied, and handed over.

Notes: A Place to Get Started on Self-Improvement

My Unpacked Suitcase

Life Lesson's Learned the Hard Way

When you find yourself in a bad spot, change it! Only you have the power; no one can do it for you. Life is never impossible. You have to find the courage to move! Find your patterns that lead to negativity and stop repeating them. Notice your own personal flaws. Pray for the strength to stop.

Get to know yourself. Make a list of what makes you *you*. Some days when it seems confusing, it's handy to look at it and remind yourself. Don't be afraid to make positive changes to this list. As we dive into God's Word, He grows us, and we may find it necessary for a new and improved list. Growth is good!

Don't deny your brokenness. Thrive in your flaws and authenticity. You be you, and let me be me! Our uniqueness is our gift; be okay with that. No one is perfect. If we were, we wouldn't have needed Jesus!

God uses the broken; no one is ever so lost that He won't use them. It's through our brokenness that someone else may be found.

Don't judge! James 4:12 says, "There is only one Lawgiver and Judge, the one who is able to save and destroy. But you—who are you to judge your neighbor?" You have no idea what someone else has dealt with. Even your friends won't tell you all their secrets and insecurities. Be careful not to think you know too much about anyone's situation. After all, how many times have you screwed up yourself?

Forgive as fast as you can! Holding on to anger is like drinking poison for you and those around you. Let that crap go or it will eat you alive and rob you of your joy. Plus, the Bible clearly says we have to forgive if we ourselves want to be forgiven.

Don't get hung up on the bad and think that one rotten season of your life has wrecked you. Nothing is unsavable for God. No act is greater or weighed in His eyes. He will redeem you if you give Him the chance. He will turn your heartache into healing if you ask for it.

When told a secret, keep it.

Don't dwell on the bad. Find the positive and stay there. Everything changes—learn to roll with it!

Be patient, little one! Every single thing happens in God's timing, not yours. So hold still and let Him be God. Free yourself from trying to do everything on your own.

Sometimes the things we don't see coming end up being the blessing we didn't know we needed! Amen.

About the Author

LynnDee lives in Asotin, Washington, with her husband Shawn. Blended together, they have one son and three daughters. She owns a salon in Clarkston, Washington, and works alongside her mom and ten amazing women. In her spare time, she enjoys adventuring in the outdoors with her husband and family. They hunt, fish, four-wheel, jet boat, and spend most weekends away at their "place of peace" in Hells Canyon.

Photographs

www.ingramcontent.com/pod-product-compliance
Ingram Content Group UK Ltd.
Pitfield, Milton Keynes, MK11 3LW, UK
UKHW042004230426
12048UKWH00009B/532